Communicating, Training, and Developing for Quality Performance

The Management Master Series

William F. Christopher
Editor-in-Chief

12

Communicating, Training, and Developing for Quality Performance

Saul W. Gellerman

PRODUCTIVITY PRESS

Portland, Oregon

Volume 12 of the *Management Master Series*.
William F. Christopher, Editor-in-Chief
Copyright © 1995 by Productivity Press, Inc.

Productivity Press
P.O. Box 13390
Portland, OR 97213-0390
United States of America
Telephone: 503-235-0600
Telefax: 503-235-0909

ISBN: 1-56327-077-3

Book and cover design by William Stanton
Cover illustration by Paul Zwolak
Typeset by Laser Words, Madras, India
Printed and bound by BookCrafters in the United States of America

Library of Congress Cataloging-in-Publication Data

Gellerman, Saul W.
     Communicating, training, and developing for quality performance /
Saul W. Gellerman.
        p.   cm. – (Management master series; v. 12)
        1. Communication in management. 2. Employees–Training of. I. Title.
II. Series.
     HD30.3.G447   1995   94-24002
     658.4′5–dc20   CIP

00 99 98 97 96 95   10 9 8 7 6 5 4 3 2 1

— CONTENTS —

PUBLISHER'S MESSAGE

The *Management Master Series* was designed to discover and disseminate to you the world's best concepts, principles, and current practices in excellent management. We present this information in a concise and easy-to-use format to provide you with the tools and techniques you need to stay abreast of this rapidly accelerating world of ideas.

World-class competitiveness requires managers today to be thoroughly informed about how and what other internationally successful managers are doing. What works? What doesn't? and Why?

Management is often considered a "neglected art." It is not possible to know how to manage before you are made a manager. But once you become a manager you are expected to know how to manage and to do it well, right from the start.

One result of this neglect in management training has been managers who rely on control rather than creativity. Certainly, managers in this century have shown a distinct neglect of workers as creative human beings. The idea that employees are an organization's most valuable asset is still very new. How managers can inspire and direct the creativity and intelligence of everyone involved in the work of an organization has only begun to emerge.

Perhaps if we consider management as a "science" the task of learning how to manage well will be easier. A scientist begins with an hypothesis and then runs experiments to observe whether the hypothesis is correct. Scientists depend on detailed notes about the experiment — the timing, the ingredients, the amounts — and carefully record all results as they test new hypotheses. Certain things come to be known by this method; for instance, that water always consists of one part oxygen and two parts hydrogen.

We as managers must learn from our experience and from the experience of others. The scientific approach provides a model for learning. Science begins with vision and desired outcomes, and achieves its purpose through observation, experiment, and analysis of precisely recorded results. And then what is newly discovered is shared so that each person's research will build on the work of others.

Our organizations, however, rarely provide the time for learning or experimentation. As a manager, you need information from those who have already experimented and learned and recorded their results. You need it in brief, clear, and detailed form so that you can apply it immediately.

It is our purpose to help you confront the difficult task of managing in these turbulent times. As the shape of leadership changes, The *Management Master Series* will continue to bring you the best learning available to support your own increasing artistry in the evolving science of management.

We at Productivity Press are grateful to William F. Christopher and our staff of editors who have searched out those masters with the knowledge, experience, and ability to write concisely and completely on excellence in management practice. We wish also to thank the individual volume authors; Diane Asay, project manager; Julie Zinkus, manuscript editor; Karen Jones, managing editor; Bill Stanton, design and production management; Susan Swanson, production coordination; Laser Words, text and graphics composition.

Norman Bodek
Publisher

Part 1
Communication

INTRODUCTION

Let's set an example of good communication right from the start, by defining not only what communication is, but also what it is not:

> *Communication* is the accurate flow of needed information between two or more persons. When that information isn't needed, it's *noise*. When it isn't interpreted accurately, it's *miscommunication*, and if it doesn't flow at all, it's *noncommunication*.

Never assume that words mean the same thing to other people that they mean to you! Rule number one for effective communication is: *always define your terms*. (See Figure 1.)

You can't manage well if you can't communicate well. It's no exaggeration to compare communication to the circulation of blood: communication is what keeps an organization alive. The reliable flow of relevant facts, figures, and ideas from person to person at the right time is *central* to everything that managers do.

Written Communication

Next time you write something that you want other people to understand and remember, think of this tried-and-true formula:

1. Tell them what you're going to tell them — a quick overview of your entire message.

2. Tell them what you told them you were going to tell them — in other words, fill in the details.

3. Tell them again what you have just told them — a summary that hammers home your main points.

Figure 1. What they hear may be different from what you mean.

WHAT'S IN THIS BOOK

Now, here's an example of the first step toward good written communication: an overview of what you'll find in the rest of this book:

- First, we'll establish the link between communication and the main theme of this series, continuous improvement. (It's a direct link, and each is vital to the other.)

- Second, we'll establish the importance of *two-way* communication. (Communication is like an electrical circuit—if the loop isn't complete, nothing happens.)

- In the next two sections we'll look at some common shortcuts to communication (memos and taping). Both are what a tennis pro calls "low-percentage shots," because they seldom work. We'll also examine two blind alleys (technology and speech writers). Both are popular but expensive methods that don't really fix many communication problems.

There are two good reasons for looking at shortcuts and blind alleys before presenting the methods that really work:

  ➤ You don't want to be tempted by those "low-percentage shots."

  ➤ The most effective ways to communicate come with a price tag attached: they're time-consuming and inconvenient. The best reason to pay that price is that in the long run, the alternatives cost even more.

Nevertheless, writing and speaking skills are useful for any manager. So we conclude these sections on speech writers (who are sometimes known as "wordsmiths") by giving away some of their professional secrets.

- Next, we'll focus on the main difference between communication methods with only a limited payoff and those that pay off very well. The less effective methods ignore the human aspect of communication: the quirky, stubborn, inattentive, and sometimes egotistical ways in which the human mind actually works. The more effective methods take those all-too-human peculiarities into account.

We'll look first into the minds of managers themselves to get some insight into why their "communication batting average" is often rather low.

After that, we'll peer into the minds of the people with whom managers try to communicate: their audience.

- Then, we'll deal with two critically important communication skills: the art of listening and the management of interpretation.

- Finally, we'll follow our own advice and end with a summary of the main points.

COMMUNICATION AND CONTINUOUS IMPROVEMENT

"Continuous improvement" means exactly what it says: it's a nonstop effort to provide better products and services at lower costs. It's the only way to maintain a competitive edge over companies that are out to grab your customers for themselves.

There are two reasons why good communication has to be at the heart of any continuous improvement process.

- To do their jobs well, people must know what's expected of them. It's up to their managers to make those expectations clear.

- This next reason is not so obvious and is related to the *continuous* aspect of continuous improvement:

    It's easier to get people to improve their work *for a short while* than to get them to *sustain* that improvement *over long periods*. To do that, you have to keep reminding them of *why* they should use new methods, since they are often less convenient than older methods.

    But those reminders become ineffective if people have to repeat them again and again. To avoid boring your audience, you continually have to find new ways to get your "old" message across.

The key to keeping your continuous improvement program alive is to keep workers focused on the right methods, and on the reasons for using them. Otherwise, they inevitably will regard the program as just another management fad: something we talk about today, and then forget about tomorrow.

TWO-WAY COMMUNICATION

Effective communication is a two-way street. It has to work well in *two* directions: from other people to you, and from you to them (See Figure 2.) Communication can't be effective if it flows in only one direction, no matter how well you manage that one-way flow. You have to manage *both* flows well.

Figure 2. Communication flows two ways. Be sure the circuit is complete.

From Other People to You

The people you communicate with interpret your message in light of what they think they *already* know about the subject of your message.

If you don't know how people feel about your message, it may make no sense to them. If so, they'll reject it, and your entire communications effort will have been wasted.

To avoid that, you have to be sure you understand *their* views before you try to communicate *yours*.

And that isn't easy, because what you think other people *said* isn't always what they *meant*. To get at meanings, you have to master one of the basic arts of communicating: *listening*.

(A little later in this book, you'll learn how to do that.)

From You to Other People

Your most carefully made plans are not going to work, if the people who have to make them work

- don't get your message in the first place

- don't think it means what you think it means

- don't remember it

- don't think it's important

This means that you have to find ways to *get your audience's attention*. It also means that you have to do more than just tell them your message. You have to *make sure* your message means the same thing to them that it does to you.

The best way to make sure that people *remember* your message is to repeat it, as often as you can. The best way to make sure people not only listen to your message, but also really *believe* it is to deliver it *personally*.

THE PROBLEM WITH SHORTCUTS

By now you can probably sense some of the costs of effective communication: It's time-consuming and it's inconvenient. That's why we're always tempted to take shortcuts with communication.

Why Shortcuts Fail

Nowadays, the two most common short-cuts are writing memos (an old shortcut), and recording speeches on videotape or audiotape (a new one).

MEMOS

The problem with memos is that most people don't read them. We scan them quickly to decide whether they are important enough to read carefully. Usually the answer is no. We simply file the memo, often in the wastebasket.

TAPED SPEECHES

The problem with taped speeches is that they are no substitute for the speaker's flesh-and-blood presence. We pay more attention to someone's live presence than to his or her image on a tape, simply because we know that a person in the same room with us may be aware of our reactions. On the other hand, a tape doesn't know (or care) if you're awake or asleep.

Also, a tape that is long enough to deal with a complicated issue is too likely to lose the attention of its audience, and one that is short enough to hold their attention probably can't explain a complicated issue.

The bottom line is that there are no *effective* short-cuts to the problems of communication. It's an inherently costly process. Many managers dislike that fact, which may be one reason why communication fails so often.

Why Talking Works

It's still true that the best way to communicate is the old-fashioned way: by talking to a few people at a time, listening to what they've got to say, and then explaining to them, as patiently as necessary, what you've got to say.

Here's why this slow, tedious method beats all of the others when it comes to getting your message across: The human mind is *prewired*, so to speak, to grasp the *meaning* of messages best when it's in direct contact with other human minds. And that, after all, is what communication is all about: *influencing other people's minds*.

Unfortunately, it isn't always easy to keep information flowing smoothly in two directions. The proof: whenever management's plans don't turn out the way they were intended to, the most common explanation for it is likely to be an all too familiar one: "We had a failure of communication."

The purpose of this book is to show you how to avoid this most common of all managerial errors. Let's start with a brief look at two strategies that are still very popular, despite the fact that they are both *unlikely* to work. Then we'll focus on the methods that *are* likely to work.

TWO BLIND ALLEYS TO AVOID

Communication failures are seldom caused by the methods we use to *transmit* messages, or by the way in which we *write* the messages themselves. Nevertheless, management often tries to prevent failures in communication by focusing on methods rather than on people. That is, they focus on what might be called the "nonhuman" aspects of the problem.

Focusing on methods usually involves

(1) trying a technological fix

(2) hiring professional speech writers (or wordsmiths) to rephrase the message itself. Both can be helpful, but they are usually less effective than dealing directly with the human causes of communication failure.

Technology in Communication

Technological advances enable us to transmit large amounts of information, almost instantaneously, all over the world — or even (literally!) out of this world. Today, much transmitted information comes in faster than most people can grasp it.

The result is *information overload*. But the bottleneck is seldom in the telecommunications equipment that sends the data or in the computers that store it. It's in the human mind itself.

The limiting factor, in other words, is no longer how much information we can send, but our ability to absorb and make sense of what is sent. That's why sending even more information, even faster than we do now, is not the answer.

So despite our high-tech advances in telecommunications, human nature causes the really tough problems in communication. And managing human nature still is, and always will be, an art, not a science. That's because so many factors are involved, and because they constantly change.

Wordsmiths

Let's face it: The English language is an inexact and unreliable medium for communicating facts and ideas. This problem affects all languages. The saving grace of English is that most other languages are even *less* precise!

The reason for the undependability of language is that the *real* meaning of words can not be found in dictionaries. Instead, real meanings are inside the heads of the people who use those words. Just because we use the same words with each other does not mean that we *think* the same things about them.

This is not to say that better writing can't improve communication. It can, and the improvement can be dramatic enough to make the effort worthwhile. Obviously, it's better if a message is clear and not convoluted; precise and not ambiguous; and lively rather than dull.

TIPS ON WRITING

Here are some tips that may help you to *write* more effectively:

Try to write as you speak. Most people have an easy, fluent speaking style that vanishes when they begin to write. It's as if speaking is *allowed* to be informal, while writing *must* be formal.

Avoid a stilted, stuffy writing style. Ask yourself, "How would I say this if I were telling it to someone?" Then write your answer down. Fix the grammar if you must, but don't change the style.

Edit what you write. Ask yourself, "How does this sound spoken aloud?" If it sounds awkward, rewrite it. If it sounds like your normal speech, with your natural phrasing, you've got it right.

Use a thesaurus. (That's a book of synonyms, sometimes available as computer software.) To express your ideas, use shorter words rather than longer ones, and common words rather than uncommon ones.

Use more periods and fewer commas. A well-written sentence usually expresses one idea, or at most, two. Also, use more paragraphs — very few paragraphs need more than three sentences.

Read your document aloud. If it sounds awkward, jarring, or dull, *rewrite* it before you send it to the printer or fax machine.

TIPS ON SPEAKING

Here are some tips that may help you to *speak* more effectively:

Never read aloud from a prepared text and never memorize a script. Most people lose all of the qualities that make their normal speech interesting (timing, emphasis, tones of voice) when reading or reciting. Instead, jot down a few key words that highlight the points you want to make. Then, just stand up and talk about them. See Figure 3 for an example.

As you speak, modulate your voice. Emphasize key words, and occasionally repeat them for added emphasis. Resist the temptation to speak as quickly as you can in order to get the speech over with. Slow down! Don't

- Last month's results
- Trends
- Opportunities
- Problems
- Corrective actions
- Teams
- Targets this month

Figure 3. Talk from a few key words, not from written text.

worry about hesitating as you find the right words. That actually makes your speech more believable, and easier to understand.

Let your audience hear you. If you don't have a microphone, project your voice so that the person who is farthest away from you can hear you clearly.

Glance at your notes only occasionally. Most of the time, look at your audience.

Always speak to *an individual* in the audience. Never "speak" at the floor or ceiling, to your notes, or to no one in particular. Instead, look at someone in the audience — anyone — and look that person straight in the eye.

Speak directly to that person for perhaps ten seconds. Then, quickly, move your gaze to another person's eyes, and speak directly to him or her. Keep shifting your gaze from person to person, periodically returning to someone you have previously "spoken" to. (See Figure 4.)

Figure 4. Shift eye contact from person to person while speaking.

Hold your audience's attention. Remember, they are watching you as well as listening to you. They are often more interested in what you look like and how you express yourself than in what you have to say. To hold their attention, move around a little — but only a little. Use your hands, as well as your voice, to emphasize your points.

Strike a balance between too much and too little movement as you speak. If you jump around too much, your audience may conclude that you are twitchy, and will begin to pay more attention to how you move than to what you say. On the other hand, if you just stand there motionless, they may conclude that since you *appear* to be uninteresting, what you have to say must also be uninteresting!

These few tips may help you to communicate more effectively. However, the words we choose and how we express than rarely causes a communication failure. Instead, the main reason for communication failures is inside people's heads. To communicate well, you have to know how to manage *attitudes*. So we now turn to the human aspect of communication, which is where we can find the real payoffs.

MANAGERS' ATTITUDES

The most important attitude you have to manage is your own. Once you get this one right, it won't be difficult to manage the other peoples' attitudes.

Managers are trained to be *efficient*, that is, to get things done at the least cost. That's usually the key to holding down expenses and pushing up productivity. But one big exception to that rule is communication.

There's not much point to being efficient if you can't also be *effective* — that is, if you can't achieve what you set out to achieve in the first place. In the case of communication, that achievement is getting people to do what you want them to do.

There are some hard truths that you have to face about effective communication. *It's inherently inefficient*. That does not necessarily mean that you have to spend a lot of money to communicate well. But if you're going to do it right, communication takes a lot of *time*. What's more, it's also *inconvenient*.

To communicate effectively, managers have to face these hard truths and learn to live with them. To communicate well, you have to spend most of your time *talking and listening* to other people. (In fact, several recent studies show that this is exactly how the most effective managers actually do their jobs.)

Make up your mind to rearrange your schedule so the people you need to communicate with have a priority claim on your time. With just that one step, you are already halfway down the road to better communication. The reason: In the real world, communication has more to do with *time management* than with acquiring a fancy vocabulary or investing in the latest technological marvels.

THE ATTITUDES OF THE AUDIENCE

In most cases, the biggest barrier to effective communication is in the minds of the people with whom we want to communicate. They may *interpret* your messages quite differently from the way you meant them. (See Figure 1.) To be sure that your attempts at communication actually work, you must actively manage that interpretation process. You have to get "inside the heads" of your audience and learn to look at the messages you are trying to send them from *their* perspective.

The first thing to remember is that you're not the only person competing for the attention of your audience. They get lots of other messages from lots of other people, and some of those messages may contradict yours. So you have to find a way to make your message more convincing, and more memorable, than the rest.

This is where time management becomes critically important. We tend to be more receptive to messages from people we know well — that is, we try harder to understand them, and interpret them more generously, than messages from strangers. (This is why many fund drives ask their volunteers to seek donations from their friends. It's harder to say no to someone you know.)

So one secret to opening up your audience to your message is to be *well known* to them. Long before you have an important message to convey, you have to cultivate them. Spend time with them, learn as much as you can about them, and try to be helpful to them.

A second secret is to see them as *frequently* as you can. If you have to choose between many short visits to a group, and a few long visits, choose many short visits. (It isn't as convenient, but it's a much more effective way to build familiarity and trust.) Always try to minimize the interval between your last visit and the next.

You'll gain another important advantage from cultivating your audience: you'll discover their *point of view*. We all look at issues from the standpoint of what we already know and believe, what we consider right and wrong, and what we think is in our self-interest. Different points of view can result in sharply different interpretations of the same message. By taking the audience's point of view into account as you prepare your message, you can avoid miscommunication. (See Figure 5.)

So the best way to get your audience's attention in the first place, and to be sure they are open to your message, is to make sure your face and your voice are familiar to them. That requires a big investment of your time. To guarantee

Figure 5. The more you *know* your people, the more they'll hear your message.

the highest possible return on that investment, you have to master an important art.

THE ART OF LISTENING

Effective listening means more than being able to repeat what someone says to you. A telephone answering machine can do that, but we don't expect the machine to *understand* us. Effective listening means being able to convince someone that we not only hear what they say, but know what they *mean*.

You can't listen effectively by listening passively (that is, by simply being aware of what someone says). Neither can you listen effectively by listening defensively (that is, by looking for defects in the other person's statements to "prove" that he is wrong and you are right).

Active Listening

The best way to listen effectively is to actively probe for meanings. You can do that by asking others to explain or clarify what they say. Remember, what other people say usually makes sense *to them*. If it doesn't make sense to you, then you are either starting from different assumptions, or they are using words that have different meanings for them than for you.

The best way to clear up these miscommunications, or better still, to avoid them altogether, is to try to rephrase what someone says to you, using your own words. Then ask that person whether your version is more or less equivalent to what they meant. If they say yes, your understanding of their meaning is about as close to being accurate as we fallible humans ever get. If they say no, keep rephrasing your interpretation until they say yes.

Respect

As you practice this art, you'll make an interesting discovery. The most reliable way to get someone to agree that you have understood them is to *start with their assumptions*, even if they are different from yours. This enables you to "see the world as they see it." When you do that, their point of view usually seems more sensible and respectable, even if (in the final analysis) you can't accept it.

But *respect* makes a big difference. In communication, as in so much of life, it's the little things that count. We read meaning into facial expressions, tones of voice, even choices of words. We decide whether to believe someone, and how much importance to give their message, more from *how* that person speaks than from what they say.

Unless you're a trained actor, it's best not to concentrate on trying to get your gestures and voice inflections

Figure 6. Listening — the first step to effective communication.

right. Instead, *get your attitudes right*. If you develop genuine respect for the opinions of others, it shows automatically in the ways you express yourself. (Unfortunately, a lack of respect shows itself just as automatically!) Therefore, indirectly, effective listening and respectful responses can make your own message more *believable*. (See Figure 6.)

MANAGING INTERPRETATION

Managing interpretation is the art of making sure that what other people think you mean matches what you think you mean. Think of it as the quality-control aspect of communication.

Three factors are involved: *context* (how people fit your message into what they already believe about the subject), *clarity* (whether they read more than one message into what you are saying), and *semantics* (what your words mean to them).

Context

We attempt to make sense of incoming messages by comparing them to information we have already received. The process is something like "filing." Unfortunately, it is all too easy to misfile the incoming message. That's because we access some of our belief systems (or "files") more easily than others.

Suppose, for example, that someone is upset about his pay. That makes the "pay file" in his head much more accessible than most other files. Almost any incoming message, including yours, could wind up being "filed" under "pay," even if it had little or nothing to do with pay. You might want to talk to this person about coffee, or the weather, or some other neutral topic, and still find yourself caught up in a hot discussion about pay!

In order to communicate effectively, you have to find out what's already of high interest to the people in your audience. The best way to do that is to *pay attention* whenever you're present at their informal conversations. The second best way is to *ask* them what's on their minds. The third best way is to ask someone who knows them well what he or she *thinks* is on their minds.

If the concerns of your audience are related to yours (for example, if they're worried about job security, and you want to talk about becoming more competitive), it won't be hard to get their attention. But if their concerns are not closely related to yours, you'll need a way to get their attention *before* you present your message.

Professional speakers have a serious reason for collecting lots of "belly-laugh" jokes: they can't get their jobs done without them. You've probably noticed that good speakers spend a few minutes "warming up" their audience, before getting down to the real substance of their talk. They want to win the attention and sympathy of their listeners. Without both, they'd find it tough to deliver the serious part of their message.

That's why, when you know that something else is on the minds of the people in your audience, you begin your talk by discussing that "something else." Only when you get their attention and sympathy do you begin turning the conversation toward your real topic.

Always show your audience the *connection* between what they want to hear and what you want to talk about. You'll get the most attention, as well as the most cooperative attitudes, when your audience realizes your message is a helpful step toward getting what they want.

Clarity

A *mixed message* can be interpreted in more than one way. It may even seem to contradict itself. It usually has two effects, neither of which is good: Some people think you can't make up your mind, and others think that one of your messages is the "real" one and the other one is "fake."

Mixed messages usually occur when managers try to reach more than one goal. Sometimes they do not make it clear that one does not have to choose between them. A classical example is quantity *vs.* quality in production. When managers stress first one of these goals, and then the other, employees may feel uncertain as to what the company really expects of them.

The solution is to present all high-priority goals together, rather than separately, *every time*. Never discuss one without at least mentioning the others. You also have to demonstrate how the company can jointly achieve all goals. The point to stress is that you always achieve priority goals *together*, never separately or at the expense of each other.

Some messages, however, are deliberately mixed. This happens when managers want to deter risky activity by employees, such as testing the limits of rules to see how much they can get away with. To deliberately mix a message, managers may purposely leave the definition of the rules fuzzy, rather than precise.

The idea is that sensible people realize that the only way to pinpoint, or locate, an indistinct "borderline" is to cross it and suffer the consequences. (This will not deter those who are "not so sensible," but there are fewer of them to deal with.)

Semantics

Semantics is concerned with meanings, or how words relate to the things they represent. Sometimes that relationship gets rather vague and fuzzy, which is why we need to study semantics in the first place.

If everyone consulted the same dictionary before they spoke, or before they decided what someone meant by a particular word, communication would be a great deal more reliable than it is. Unfortunately, most people seldom bother to use dictionaries, or do so as a last, desperate resort.

Since that is the case, there's an uncomfortable fact that we have to face: *Language is really a code*. It's a collection of words that stand for many different things. The problem is that each of us interprets the code with our own private code book, which may or may not correspond to anyone else's code book. (See Figure 7.)

So even when you and someone else use the same words, you may be referring to quite different things. The only code book that is the same for everyone is the one

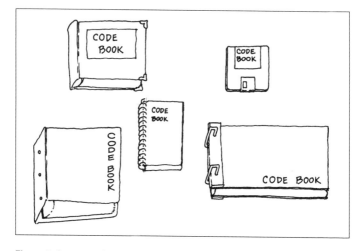

Figure 7. Language is a code — and everyone's code book is different.

we seldom use: the dictionary. That, in a nutshell, is why misunderstandings are so common.

Nevertheless, here are some rules that can help you convey your thoughts more accurately:

Jargon is a technical vocabulary. Usually only professionals understand the meaning of jargon. The rule here is simple: for good communication, use jargon only with other professionals, never with laymen.

Slang is an informal language. It is usually temporary (or "trendy"), and usually only people in a particular group understand it. (For example, teenagers continually create new slang, quickly replacing it with even newer slang.) The rule is the same: never use slang with someone who is not a member of the group in which it is used. In particular, never use slang with foreigners — it usually leaves them baffled.

Express yourself with simple, common words. However, if you must use an uncommon word, always *define* it promptly, by translating it into more ordinary language.

Strike a balance between being too *terse* and being too *talkative*:

- If what you say is too condensed, people use their own imaginations to fill in the details. And, their imaginations may lead them far away from what you intended.

- If what you say is too lengthy and detailed, some people may become so involved in the small points that they lose sight of your overall purpose. (We say that they "can't see the forest for the trees.") Others get bored and let their attention drift.

It's best to start with only a moderate amount of detail, and then *test* their grasp of your message. Ask them to express, in their own words, what they think you mean. That way you'll know whether you need to add more detail, and how much. Here's an example. You might say:

> "This project is our top priority for today. If necessary, you can postpone work on other projects so you can concentrate on this one. If this conflicts with any other priorities that you're working on, please see me. Any questions?"

To check on whether your message got across accurately, ask for *restatements*. For example, you might say:

> "Just to be sure we all understand this in the same way, I'm going to ask some of you to rephrase my statement in your own words. John, what do you think I meant?"

John might say:

> "I think you mean that we are to stop work on everything else and work full-time on this new priority job."

To which you might reply:

"Well, I'm glad you said that, because it shows I didn't express myself as clearly as I wanted to. John, I want you to stop working only on your *nonpriority* tasks and use only that time to work on the new job. But the new job does not push aside any existing priority jobs. Is that clearer, John?"

John might say:

"I think I've got it. To open up time for the new job, we temporarily drop all nonpriority work. Today is strictly for priority jobs. We'll get back to the nonpriority jobs tomorrow, after we finish this new job."

To which you might reply:

"John, you've got it. That's exactly right."

Never assume that because the precise meaning of a message is clear to you, it is necessarily clear to others. Good communication is as much a matter of *testing* other people's grasp of what you meant, and of *correcting* your mistakes, as it is expressing yourself *clearly* in the first place.

SUMMARY

Now, let's review the main points:

1. Define your terms. Always make sure your audience knows what you are talking about. Whenever you use an uncommon word, or a common word in an uncommon sense, *define* it.

2. Repeat an important message three times.

> ➤ Outline it.

> ➤ Fill in the details.

➤ Summarize the main points.

3. Avoid shortcuts. They may save time, but they don't get your message across. Effective communication takes time, period.

4. Beware of blind alleys. They can cost lots of money, but yield only marginal improvements in *understanding* and *action*, which are what communication is all about.

5. Recognize that effective communication is a two-way street. Listening is just as important as telling.

6. Write as you speak. Try to make your writing as *conversational* as possible. Good writing is easy to read. Good speaking is easy to listen to.

7. Recognize that effective communication is inherently inefficient and inconvenient. That's the bad news. The good news is that it more than pays for itself in improved performance, better control, and better morale.

8. To communicate better, spend more time with your people. Effective communication has more to do with how you manage your time than with your vocabulary or with technology.

9. To *listen* effectively, probe for what people mean. Try rephrasing what they say to see if they agree that you understood them.

10. Get your attitude right. The right attitude is even more important than the right gestures or voice inflections. Learn to respect your audience. It makes them more receptive to your message.

11. Know what interests your audience. To get your message across, first find out what already interests your audience and tie your message to that.

12. Avoid sending mixed messages. Discuss all priority goals together. Never discuss them separately.

13. Avoid slang or jargon. Don't assume anyone, especially a foreigner, is familiar with it.

14. Never assume your message is clear to others. *Test* their grasp of what you meant. If they don't get it, correct your message — and keep correcting it, as long as necessary, until they get it.

Part 2
Training and Development

INTRODUCTION

Training is the process of teaching new skills to someone else. You can't have training without having someone who teaches: a trainer or a "trainer-substitute," such as a textbook or a videotape. Training usually takes place in a classroom specially equipped for that purpose, and trainers usually follow a planned course of instruction.

Development is the process of learning from your own experience. It could also be called "self-education." It is seldom planned, does not require a trainer, and can occur anywhere — often unexpectedly. Unfortunately, it sometimes doesn't occur at all.

Training occurs occasionally and tends to be brief, while development is ongoing. There are many more opportunities for development to occur by itself than for training to be scheduled, organized, paid for, and presented.

One of the main functions of training is to prepare people for development. Training enables people to learn as much as possible on the job *after* the training. Many people eventually learn far more on the job than they do from training. For most, however, training is a necessary first step toward development.

The distinction between these two learning processes is not absolute. For example, a *mentor*, who does not follow a planned course of instruction, may help you to learn more from your own experience than you could by yourself. That case would fit the definition of both training *and* development.

Both training and development help people become more *competent* in their work. Because their definitions overlap somewhat, and also because they lead to the same result, it makes sense to consider training and development together.

We'll begin this review by looking at five reasons why training and development are important to any organization committed to continuous improvement. Then we'll consider the vital role of *timing* in determining the outcome of both of these processes.

Next we'll look specifically at *training* and consider two factors that strongly influence its results: time and space. We'll complete our review of training by considering how trainers can organize the material for maximum effectiveness.

Our review of the *development* process will emphasize the importance of "being in the right place at the right time," and of having a prepared mind. To some extent, a company can manage both of these requirements rather than leave them to chance. We'll also consider the role of mentors.

We'll close with a summary of the main points on both training and development.

THE IMPORTANCE OF TRAINING AND DEVELOPMENT

Training and development are the primary methods by which companies can make their own people *more productive*, and thereby *add value* to them. But these two processes have at least five other advantages, as well:

Recruiting. A good training program attracts ambitious job-seekers. Companies that offer such programs get more high-quality applicants, so they can hire more *selectively* than their competitors can. This enables them to continually upgrade the quality and potential of the organization.

Promotion-from-within. Companies with good development and training programs can keep their managerial pipeline filled with people who are qualified for higher-level jobs. This reduces their need to bring in high-level executives from outside the firm.

Job burn-out. Anyone who does the same job for an extended period of time may tire of it and lose interest. Of course, burn-out effectively blocks continuous improvement for the affected individual. Fortunately, well-timed training programs can help to avert this common problem.

Change. Technological or organizational change can have the unfortunate effect of making some people obsolete or redundant. They become liabilities rather than assets. The best way to avoid both problems is through training and development.

Turnover. Ambitious, high-potential employees may leave a firm if their pathway to promotion is blocked. Well-planned development programs can help to retain these valuable human assets.

TIMING

Many factors influence the effectiveness of both training and development. By far, the most important of these is *timing*.

For training to be effective, a company must provide it when employees are *ready* for it, and can *practice* what they learn immediately afterward.

- Training usually presumes that employees already have certain skills, such as math or English, that they will need in the training course itself. Training may also presume that employees are familiar with certain tools or terminology. If they are not, they need to learn those essentials *first*. Otherwise, training will be a waste of time.

- People who mastered their jobs long ago, and have not learned many new skills since then, often find it hard to benefit from a training program. The best way to deal with this problem is to *prevent* it with periodic refresher courses or broadening courses.

The second-best way is to train such people *separately* from those who were trained more recently. In this case, lengthen the course to give them more *time* to learn.

Scheduling Training

Is there a best time for training, when employees can gain the most from it? Yes, but it isn't always practical to schedule training that way. People benefit most from training given within one or two years of when their learning curves from previous training begin to level off.

The learning curve in Figure 8 shows the typical rate at which people master new information or new skills. After a slow start, in which they accustom themselves to the new material (A), learning speeds up rapidly (B), but then begins to slow down (C). Depending on the difficulty of the material they're learning, it may take a year or two to get through both phase A and phase B. The best time to start someone with new or advanced training is, roughly, one to two years into phase C.

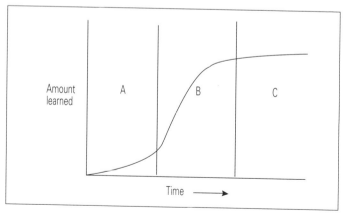

Figure 8. Typical Learning Curve

As a rule, such rapid transitions from one training program to another are rare. They usually occur only when the company itself is growing very fast. In most companies, the transition from job to job is much slower.

As a result, many people going into their second or third training program have already moved quite far into phase *c* and may be overripe. That is, they may no longer be as comfortable with the learning process as they once were, and therefore may be less eager to try it. However, some companies avoid this problem by providing some form of training to all employees at least annually, often as part of TQM development. The idea is to maintain the individual's *readiness to learn*. When training occurs this often, the individual is actually on *several* learning curves at the same time. (See Figure 9.)

No training program can guarantee, by itself, that trainees will remember what they learned. Only *practice* can do that. For employees to get the most out of training a company must immediately offer opportunities for them

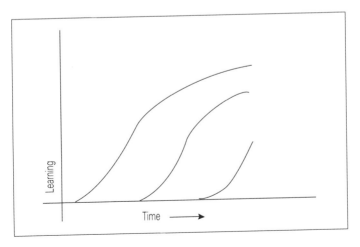

Figure 9. Simultaneous Learning Curves

to use the newly-learned skills on the job. Coordinating training with scheduled changes in job assignments also helps to prevent wasted effort.

Timing also influences development. People who have done the same job for a long time (more than five or six years) may find it difficult to make the transition to a new assignment. Also, executives who rate their promotion prospects may perceive them as being limited to their present roles, even when they still have the potential to learn new roles.

Planning Training and Development

The effect of timing on the outcomes of training and development is too important to be left to chance. Both should be *programmed* at least five years ahead, at least for those managers, professionals, and key employees who are judged to offer the most valuable potential to their firms.

Effective training and development require continual management by someone who reports directly to a high-level executive. In larger firms, this should be the Chief Human Resources Officer. In medium-sized and smaller firms, it should be the Chief Executive Officer.

Next, let's take an in-depth look at some of the key factors that determine the outcome of *training*.

TRAINING: THE TIME AND SPACE FACTORS

Here are some guidelines for setting up a successful training session:

Divide training courses into a series of relatively short sessions. Usually, one-and-a-half hours is about as long as a session should last. Longer sessions run the risk of fatigue, restlessness, and loss of attention.

Schedule about four such sessions per day. To plan on more than four sessions is to run the same risks as for overly long sessions. The human mind (and the human capacity for sitting still) can absorb only so much.

Diversify the method of instruction to maintain student interest throughout each session. Ideally, trainers should present no more than half of each session themselves. (Ninety minutes is a long time to listen to a lecture or watch a demonstration!)

Involve students in about half of each session. Have small groups discuss the material just presented by the trainer or practice techniques he or she has demonstrated, or both.

Use audio-visual aids to help diversify the training experience. However, they should not take more than about one-third to one-half of the time available in any given session.

Vary the methods you use to present information. Use lectures, demonstrations, discussion groups, practice groups, and audio-visual aids. Change to a new method *before* people tire of the previous one. Too much uninterrupted use of *any* method is not effective.

Design classrooms that easily encourage eye contact and interaction between the trainer and the trainees, and between the trainees themselves. *Minimize the distance* between the trainer and the trainees. The idea is to use physical closeness to encourage interaction between everyone in the classroom, and to maintain a high level of attention.

Arrange trainees' desks in an "inverted U," with the instructor at the open end. One such layout can accommodate about twelve trainees. (See Figure 10.) To accommodate up to thirty trainees, add another concentric "U" outside the first.

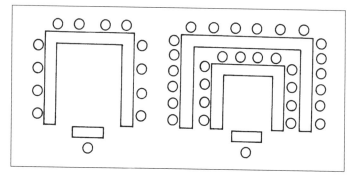

Figure 10. Ideal Classroom Layouts for Training

The advantages of this layout are:

- All of the trainees are close enough to the trainer to receive personalized attention.

- The trainer can easily tell whether trainees are attentive and understand the material being presented.

- The trainees can readily engage in discussions with each other.

Avoid the traditional classroom seating arrangement. In that arrangement, only people in the first few rows are close to the trainer. Also, most of the trainees are isolated from both the instructor and their fellow classmates, due to lack of eye contact.

The *optimum* number of trainees in a class, where teaching effectiveness and economic efficiency are balanced, is about twenty. To bring more than thirty people into a classroom defeats one of the main purposes of training, which is to give each person enough access to the trainer to ensure a good learning outcome.

TRAINING: GUIDELINES FOR COURSE MATERIAL

Here are some guidelines for deciding how to organize the material to present in a training course:

Don't overload any session with too much material. It's easy to do that when the material is familiar to you, but unfamiliar to the students. They'll need time to get used to it. Plan to invest at least five minutes in presenting each major point, including lecture, demonstration, and time for answering questions. For a complex point, or a very important one, ten minutes would be better.

Make sure trainees can see how any part of the course material fits in with the rest of the course. Give them a general outline at the beginning, so they can see "where they're going." As you present the material, refer back often to material that has already been covered.

Each new course should include both a *review* of previously presented coursework and an introduction to *new* material.

Don't wait until the end of the course to tie everything together. Do that periodically throughout the course, pulling together the points that have been made up to that point.

Provide time for supervised practice. Let trainees practice what they're learning under the watchful eye of the trainer. If all of their practice comes after the course is over, mistakes are likely. Even well-trained students need to be *confident* that they're doing the new task in the right way.

Involve the trainees in the learning process. Don't just tell them everything. Instead, ask questions to see if they already know the answers, or can figure them out for themselves. Make the trainees *work* in order to learn. Don't let them just sit passively, listening or making notes.

Some students prefer to sit silently, hoping you won't notice them. To be sure they are learning, draw them out. Ask them questions. Don't always wait for volunteers. Put some questions directly to individuals, especially those who don't volunteer.

DEVELOPMENT

Development occurs when, by ourselves, we extend our knowledge or skills beyond their previous limits. We can do this by *connecting* old information to newly-acquired information, or by *seeing* a previously unnoticed connection between existing pieces of information.

Sometimes we make these connections as a result of painstaking analysis. More often, however, they occur suddenly, when we are struck by the way in which the pieces of information fit together, and help to explain each other.

Two factors largely determine whether these insights occur as a result of on-the-job experience. The first is being in the right place at the right time. The second is having a *prepared mind*.

Right Place, Right Time

Insights are more likely to occur when we are looking at information that is *different* from the facts that we are accustomed to. This means that people whose jobs provide *varied* experience are more likely to grow, in the sense of becoming more capable, than people whose jobs involve little change.

The *right place* for development is anywhere that you are not too familiar with. The *right time* is before you get too far along in phase C of your most recent learning curve.

This has practical implications for planning career assignments, especially for *management development*. A major purpose of management development is to encourage *self-development*. That's why people who show potential for high-level positions should have opportunities to move up the promotion ladder quickly, at least *initially*, so they can start developing rapidly.

Later the rate of promotion can slow down somewhat to allow them to develop some *depth*. Meanwhile, it also helps to give them *cross-functional* assignments. These involve both line and staff jobs, and various functions within each of them.

Prepared Mind

Two qualities mark the mind of someone who is likely to grow as a result of his or her own experience. One is *knowing what to look for*. The other is *aggressively looking for it*.

KNOW WHAT TO LOOK FOR

It is usually not difficult to find what you need, if you *know* what to look for. First *define* the key problems that you face, then determine the missing pieces that would solve those problems, *if* you could find them. This alerts you to clues about where those missing pieces might be. *Informed alertness* makes a big difference in your ability to find what you need.

Consider a good infielder on a baseball team. Before each pitch, he decides what to do if the ball should be hit toward him: throw it to first base, tag the runner, or any of his many other options. He makes his decisions *before* the action takes place. Similarly, if you decide in advance what to watch for, you'll probably recognize the value of an important clue when you see it.

Some people confuse this ability to find answers with luck. Luck is really more a matter of taking *advantage* of opportunities that present themselves than of getting more than your fair share of opportunities. You can "make yourself lucky" by knowing what to look for.

LOOK AGGRESSIVELY FOR CLUES

Looking aggressively requires a conscious determination to keep the needed information close to the top of your priority list. While you do your regular work, stay aware and open to new information. It may take weeks or even months to find the clues and facts, but for as long as it takes, keep looking.

The discoveries that lead to enhanced abilities sometimes occur at the very moment you run into the facts that you need. But they can also occur afterward, when the meaning of those facts sinks in. They can even occur in your sleep! When you have been working on a problem for a long time, you literally may wake up in the middle of the night with a clear answer to it.

MENTORS

A mentor is an advisor who helps you sort out the problems you are working on, and tries to bring you the perspective of his or her long experience. Typically, a mentor is an older executive who has already dealt with problems similar to those you face. Mentors can be very helpful in the development process, especially with younger managers.

It is important for mentors to be both objective and nonthreatening. They should not have executive authority over the manager they are advising and should not evaluate the manager's work. Otherwise, it would be difficult for the manager to confide in the mentor to the extent needed to make their relationship fruitful.

The main value of a mentor is in providing a sounding board for the manager as he or she works toward the solution of the various problems. Mentors can help managers clarify issues; they can play devil's advocate to help managers assess the strengths and weaknesses of the various positions they might take; and they can provide useful second opinions on many of the issues that managers face. When managers regard them as both well-informed and objective, mentors can be especially useful.

SUMMARY

- One of the main functions of training is to prepare people to learn as much as possible from events that occur on the job *after* they complete the training itself.

- Training and development are ways of *adding value* to the people in an organization by:

  ➤ enabling companies to hire more *selectively*

  ➤ enabling them to promote more people from within

  ➤ avoiding *burn-out*

  ➤ helping people to adjust to *change*

  ➤ minimizing *turnover*

- *Timing* is the most important factor that influences the effectiveness of both training and development. Therefore, plan training and development at least five years ahead for those people who appear to offer the most potential to their firms.

- Always vary the method by which you present information in training sessions. Too much uninterrupted use of *any* method is likely to be ineffective.

- Design classrooms for easy *eye contact* between the trainer and trainees, and between the trainees themselves.

- The *optimum* number of trainees in a training class is about twenty. The *maximum* number for training effectiveness is about thirty.

- Self-development occurs when we are struck by the way in which pieces of information fit together, or help to explain each other.

- To encourage self-development, allow high-potential people to move up the promotion ladder quickly, at least initially. Later, slow down the promotion rate to give them time to develop some depth.

- You can "make yourself lucky" by knowing what to look for.

- The discoveries that lead to enhanced abilities can occur at the moment one encounters critical facts, or afterward — even while one is asleep!

- Mentors who are regarded as well-informed and objective can have a positive effect on the development of an individual manager's abilities.

BIBLIOGRAPHY

PART 1. COMMUNICATION

Kaplan, R.F., W.H. Drath, and J.R. Kofodimos, "Why Some Managers Don't Get the Message." *Across the Board* (September 1985): 63–69.

Lengel, R.H., and R.L. Daft, "The Selection of Communications Media as an Executive Skill." *The Academy of Management Executive* (August, 1988): 225–232.

Luthans, F., and J.K. Larsen, "How Managers Really Communicate." *Human Relations* 39, no. 2 (1986): 161–178.

PART 2. TRAINING AND DEVELOPMENT

Kaye, B. "Career Development Puts Training in Its Place." *Personnel Journal* (February 1983): 132–137.

McCall, M.W. Jr., M.M. Lombardo, and A.M. Morrison. *The Lessons of Experience: How Successful Executives Develop on the Job.* Lexington, Mass.: D.C. Heath (1988).

Wilson, J.A., and N.S. Elman, "Organizational Benefits of Mentoring." *The Academy of Management Executive* (November, 1991): 84–94.

ABOUT THE AUTHOR

Saul W. Gellerman is a management consultant, specializing in executive development and organization studies. He is the author of nine books, including *Motivation and Productivity* and *Motivation in the Real World*, and *Motivating Superior Performance*, volume 5 of the *Management Master Series*. He was formerly dean of the Graduate School of Management at the University of Dallas. Dr. Gellerman is based in Irving, Texas.

The Management Master Series

The *Management Master Series* offers business managers leading-edge information on the best contemporary management practices. Written by highly respected authorities, each short "briefcase book" addresses a specific topic in a concise, to-the-point presentation, using both text and illustrations. These are ideal books for busy managers who want to get the whole message quickly.

Set 1 — Great Management Ideas

1. *Management Alert: Don't Reform—Transform!*
    Michael J. Kami

    Transform your corporation: adapt faster, be more productive, perform better.

2. *Vision, Mission, Total Quality: Leadership Tools for Turbulent Times*
    William F. Christopher

    Build your vision and mission to achieve world class goals.

3. *The Power of Strategic Partnering*
    Eberhard E. Scheuing

    Take advantage of the strengths in your customer-supplier chain.

4. *New Performance Measures*
    Brian H. Maskell

    Measure service, quality, and flexibility with methods that address your customers' needs.

5. *Motivating Superior Performance*
    Saul W. Gellerman

    Use these key factors—nonmonetary as well as monetary—to improve employee performance.

6. *Doing and Rewarding: Inside a High-Performance Organization*
    Carl G. Thor

    Design systems to reward superior performance and encourage productivity.

PRODUCTIVITY PRESS, Dept. BK, PO Box 13390, Portland, OR 97213-0390
Phone (503) 235-0600   Fax (503) 235-0909

Set 2 — Total Quality

7. *The 16-Point Strategy for Productivity and Total Quality*
   William F. Christopher and Carl G. Thor
   Essential points you need to know to improve the performance of your organization.

8. *The TQM Paradigm: Key Ideas That Make It Work*
   Derm Barrett
   Get a firm grasp of the world-changing ideas behind the Total Quality movement.

9. *Process Management: A Systems Approach to Total Quality*
   Eugene H. Melan
   Learn how a business process orientation will clarify and streamline your organization's capabilities.

10. *Practical Benchmarking for Mutual Improvement*
    Carl G. Thor
    Discover a down-to-earth approach to benchmarking and building useful partnerships for quality.

11. *Mistake-Proofing: Designing Errors Out*
    Richard B. Chase and Douglas M. Stewart
    Learn how to eliminate errors and defects at the source with inexpensive poka-yoke devices and staff creativity.

12. *Communicating, Training, and Developing for Quality Performance*
    Saul W. Gellerman
    Gain quick expertise in communication and employee development basics.

These books are sold in sets. Each set is $85.00 plus $5.00 shipping and handling. Future sets will cover such topics as Customer Service, Leadership, and Innovation. For complete details, call 800-394-6868 or fax 800-394-6286.

PRODUCTIVITY PRESS, Dept. BK, PO Box 13390, Portland, OR 97213-0390
Phone (503) 235-0600   Fax (503) 235-0909

BOOKS FROM PRODUCTIVITY PRESS

Productivity Press provides individuals and companies with materials they need to achieve excellence in quality, productivity, and the creative involvement of all employees. Through sets of learning tools and techniques, Productivity supports continuous improvement as a vision, and as a strategy. Many of our leading-edge products are direct source materials translated into English for the first time from industrial leaders around the world. Call toll-free 1-800-394-6868 for our free catalog.

Feedback Toolkit
16 Tools for Better Communication in the Workplace
Rick Maurer
In companies striving to reduce hierarchy and foster trust and responsible participation, good person-to-person feedback can be as important as sophisticated computer technology in enabling effective teamwork. Feedback is an important map of your situation, a way to tell whether you are "on or off track." Used well, feedback can motivate people to their highest level of performance. Despite its significance, this level of information sharing makes most managers uncomfortable. *Feedback Toolkit* addresses this natural hesitation with an easy-to-grasp 6-step framework and 16 practical and creative approaches for giving and receiving feedback with individuals and groups. Maurer's reality-tested methods in *Feedback Toolkit* are indispensable equipment for managers and teams in every organization.
ISBN 1-56327-056-0 / 109 pages / $15.00 / Order FEED-B247

The Teamwork Advantage
An Inside Look at Japanese Product and Technology Development
Jeffrey L. Funk
How are so many Japanese manufacturing firms shortening product time-to-market, reducing costs, and improving quality? The answer is teamwork. Dr. Funk spent 18 months as a visiting engineer at Mitsubishi and Yokogawa Hokushin Electric and knows firsthand how Japanese corporate culture promotes effective teamwork in production, design, and technology development. Here's a penetrating case study and analysis that presents a truly viable model for the West.
ISBN 1-915299-69-0 / 508 pages / $50.00 / Order TEAMAD-B247

PRODUCTIVITY PRESS, Dept. BK, PO Box 13390, Portland, OR 97213-0390
Phone (503) 235-0600   Fax (503) 235-0909

A New American TQM
Four Practical Revolutions in Management
Shoji Shiba, Alan Graham, and David Walden
For TQM to succeed in America, you need to create an American-style "learning organization" with the full commitment and understanding of senior managers and executives. Written expressly for this audience, *A New American TQM* offers a comprehensive and detailed explanation of TQM and how to implement it, based on courses taught at MIT's Sloan School of Management and the Center for Quality Management, a consortium of American companies. Full of case studies and amply illustrated, the book examines major quality tools and how they are being used by the most progressive American companies today.
ISBN 1-56327-032-3 / 606 pages / $50.00 / Order NATQM-B247

40 Years, 20 Million Ideas
The Toyota Suggestion System
Yuzo Yasuda
This fascinating book describes how Toyota generated tremendous employee involvement in their creative idea suggestion system. It reviews the program's origins, toyota's internal promotion of the system, and examples of actual suggestions and how they were used. Personal accounts and anecdotes flavor the text and address problems encountered and their resolutions.
ISBN 1-915299-74-7 / 208 pages / $40.00 / Order 4020-B247

TO ORDER: Write, phone, or fax Productivity Press, Dept. BK, P.O. Box 13390, Portland, OR 97213-0390, phone 1-800-394-6868, fax 1-800-394-6286. Send check or charge to your credit card (American Express, Visa, MasterCard accepted).

U.S. ORDERS: Add $5 shipping for first book, $2 each additional for UPS surface delivery. We offer attractive quantity discounts for bulk purchases of individual titles; call for more information.

INTERNATIONAL ORDERS: Write, phone, or fax for quote and indicate shipping method desired. For international callers, telephone number is 503-235-0600 and fax number is 503-235-0909. Prepayment in U.S. dollars must accompany your order (checks must be drawn on U.S. banks). When quote is returned with payment, your order will be shipped promptly by the method requested.

NOTE: Prices are in U.S. dollars and are subject to change without notice.

PRODUCTIVITY PRESS, Dept. BK, PO Box 13390, Portland, OR 97213-0390
Phone (503) 235-0600   Fax (503) 235-0909